COPIA

COPIA

Poems by

ERIKA MEITNER

American Poets Continuum Series, No. 144

BOA EDITIONS, LTD. ★ ROCHESTER, NY ★ 2014

First Edition

For information about permission to reuse any material from this book please contact The Permissions Company at www.permissionscompany.com or e-mail permdude@eclipse.net.

Publications by BOA Editions, Ltd.—a not-for-profit corporation under section 501 (c) (3) of the United States Internal Revenue Code—are made possible with funds from a variety of sources, including public funds from the New York State Council on the Arts, a state agency; the Literature Program of the National Endowment for the Arts; the County of Monroe, NY; the Lannan Foundation for support of the Lannan Translations Selection Series; the Mary S. Mulligan Charitable Trust; the Rochester Area Community Foundation; the Arts & CulturalCouncil for Greater Rochester; the Steeple-Jack Fund; the Ames-Amzalak Memorial Trust in memory of Henry Ames, Semon Amzalak and Dan Amzalak; and contributions from many individuals nationwide. See Colophon on page 104 for special individual acknowledgments.

ART WORKS.
arts.gov

State of the Arts

NYSCA

Cover Design: Sandy Knight
Interior Design and Composition: Richard Foerster
Manufacturing: Bookmobile
BOA Logo: Mirko

Library of Congress Cataloging-in-Publication Data

Meitner, Erika, 1975–
  [Poems. Selections]
  Copia / by Erika Meitner. — First edition.
      pages ; cm
  ISBN 978-1-938160-46-2 (paperback) — ISBN 978-1-938160-47-9 (ebook)
  I. Title.
  PS3613.E436A6 2014
  811'.6—dc23
                                    2014005049

BOA Editions, Ltd.
250 North Goodman Street, Suite 306
Rochester, NY 14607
www.boaeditions.org
A. Poulin, Jr., Founder (1938–1996)

Contents

✦

copia, n.

Pronunciation: /ˈkəʊpɪə/
Etymology: Latin; = plenty.

Plenty, a plentiful supply: now chiefly in the Latin phrase *copia verborum,* abundance of words, a copious vocabulary. Also the Roman goddess of wealth or plenty.

a. Plenty, abundance, a copious quantity.
b. Fullness, plenitude. Obs.
c. esp. of language: Copiousness, abundance, fullness, richness.

1713   J. Addison in <u>Guardian</u> 8 Sept. 1/2   Since they [*sc.* women] have . . .such a *Copia Verborum*, or plenty of Words, 'tis Pity they should not put it to some Use.

I

Litany of Our Radical Engagement with the Material World

Objects around us are emitting light, transgressing,
                    are discrete
                    repositories—
                    tropes, backdrops, ruination, lairs.

Objects around us are blank and seamless,
                    suffer from an arbitrariness,
                    are habitual or habitually
                                        absconding.

Objects around us can be carefully etched
                              or stitched on top of our skins,
                    dismantled and placed in the trunk of a cab.

Objects around us are Oh my God.

Objects around us shimmer in air-colored suits,
                        in flesh-colored suits,
                    are waiting to be caressed.
                        They breakdance when we turn away.

Objects around us depend on fracture and fragment,
                    are picked clean, derelict—
                    shudder
                        like hostages without blindfolds
                    or tout survivability
           by trilling in the wet grass.

Objects around us are durable,
                        glow relentlessly
                    as if they're actually immortal.

Objects around us are not strangers.
                        They are the ruins
                        in which we drown.

Objects around us are expecting again,
                  blanket things with feathers
        to offer refuge
                but tremble anyway.

Objects around us wrap us in compassion,
                  sing an ode to something,
        take the long way home.

Objects around us are no substitute for anything.
Objects around us moan.

Objects around us wander the aisles,
                  take everything of worth,
                flee, exit, make off, vamoose.

Objects around us dismantle the city.
The doors are wide open. Go in.

Niagara

White towels folded into swans
       with heads touching—
              their hearted bodies trail

the floral bedspread: polyester,
       used over and over again.
              The bed itself casts a shadow

on desolate paneling.
       O bed. O motel. O girl
              in white pants—you are voluminous

and shine like the glossed doors
       on rows of identical love shacks
              punctuated with all-weather

lawn chairs out front.
       Clouds ride past the pool,
              faces of brick, the oil stains

on parking lot asphalt.
       Did someone teach you
              to park in a place like this,

between two white parallel
       lines stretched like arms
              saying come here? In the grass

behind the dumpster you lay
       your head on his pale, shirtless
              chest. On his skin, warm as

melted butter. It is the blue hour,
       floating on quiet water, after
              the sun sets, before dark.

Love on damp pavement. Love
     with sanitized glasses wrapped
         in paper. Love in the violent mist.

In the velvet night. He kisses
     the soles of your feet. O girl
         in white. Be good and take care.

I haven't fallen like that in a very long time.

Big Box Encounter

My student sends letters to me with the lights turned low.
They feature intricate vocabulary, like *soporific* and *ennui*.

Like *intervening* and *kinetic* and *tumult*. He strings words together
like he's following a difficult knitting pattern. He is both more

and less striking without a shirt on. I know this from the time
I ran into him at Walmart buying tiki torches and margarita mix

and, flustered, I studied the white floor tiles, the blue plastic
shopping cart handle, while he told me something that turned

to white noise and I tried not to look at his beautiful terrible chest,
the V-shaped wings of his chiseled hipbones. I write him back.

I tell him there are two horses outside my window and countless weeds.
I tell him that the train comes by every other hour and rattles the walls.

But how to explain my obsession with destruction? Not self-immolation,
but more of a disintegration, slow, like Alka-Seltzer in water. Like sugar in water.

I dissolve. He writes *enthralling*. He writes *epiphany* and *coffee machine*.
He is working in an office, which might as well be outer space.

I am in the mountains. The last time I worked in an office, he was ten.
I was a typewriter girl. I was a maternity-leave replacement for a fancy secretary.

I helped sell ads at TV Guide. I was fucking a guy who lived in a curtain-free studio
above a neon BAR sign on Ludlow Street and all night we were bathed in pot smoke

and flickering electric pink light. Here, the sun goes down in the flame
of an orange heat-wave moon. The train thrums and rattles the distance,

and I think of his chest with the rounded tattoo in one corner and my youth,
the hollows of his hipbones holding hard, big-box fluorescent light.

CORRESPONDENCE

I drive around in my small, old Honda Civic
and play music that reminds me of driving
the same car when it was new but no larger.

The Civic held four people, but now, with the car seat
and its five-point safety harness, it holds three.
There are Goldfish crackers ground into the floor mats.

My husband is the bassist in a local bar band.
They play classic rock covers, and though my husband
hates classic rock, he loves his powder-blue bass.

He loves playing in a band. He loves when Frank,
the owner of the bar, gets drunk and tells the band
how much he loves them. They have a monthly gig.

He makes fifty dollars a night when he plays 622.
There are things that are broken beyond repair,
but my marriage isn't one of them.

I am not telling you any of this.
Everything I am telling you is in that letter.
I will not tell you about the fact that I thought

praying mantises were an endangered species
when I was a kid. That was in the seventies.
If I think too much about my childhood,

I will feel too old to write you a letter.
The Internet tells me that this is a long-standing
urban legend; killing a praying mantis was never

illegal or subject to a fine. The origin of the myth
is unknown. Mantises are beneficial to gardens they live in.
Here it seems to make sense to evoke Eden,

but I won't. My son loves praying mantises.
He goes outside each night after dinner to *look for guys*,
and finds them tucked into the spiky barberry bushes.

I will not write you about my son, and if I mention
Eden, it would be to tell you that there's no such thing.
That you are not the talking snake and I am not

the woman without clothes who offers and offers.
The apple has no knowledge to give us. Our cosmogony
is unclear. This is not a love note, or a prayer,

or a field equation. I hold my cards close to the vest.
You send me a picture of a tattoo you'd like to get
of a compass, and the road unravels in front of my Civic

like a spool of thread. We are a gravitational singularity,
a theory that implicates epistemology, but I am not
rigorous enough in my approach to uncover anything.

You write me a letter.
I write you a letter back.
We go on like this for some time.

with/out

after Janice N. Harrington

And the mornings were detritus,
bent bottle caps, chrome diner matchbooks,

always the pack of playing cards in cellophane
with the tab half-pulled, and the unearthed voice

of the drive-thru pricked by shined key chains
jangling like tire irons. And the nights were detritus,

expired gas station receipts, mall vapors, a half-used
tin of tattoo salve, all of Bayonne, New Jersey

mapped on your back in chalk. The moon was detritus,
shining on a pickup dodging the curb, trailing nail clippings,

onion skins, translucent stars, five beat-down Nikes
that wound up phone-pole hopping in Ditmas.

And you were the detritus of magnifying glasses,
half-done lanyards, award ribbons fluttering

like condom wrappers at the shore, the wreckage
of contour lines, a hand-tooled leather souvenir

from a red rock abyss. The scent of your drawer
was fresh rubber and guitar picks, the metallurgy

of scattered loose change and blood. Your bed
wore charcoal detritus, lip-gloss and pot-dust,

ill-fitted sheets. And the detritus the July heat let loose:
gnawed Bic pen caps, a glowing Duncan Hines yo-yo

tangled in dead 9-volt connectors and envelopes
whose lips sealed shut from humidity that swelled

the windows into their frames. If you had scrawled
something on the inside of my wrist back then

it might have been a Venn diagram: your contented breath,
six glove-box necessities, the muffled places detritus would take us.

STAKING A CLAIM

It seems a certain fear underlies everything.
If I were to tell you something profound
it would be useless, as every single thing I know
is not timeless. I am particularly risk-averse.

I choose someone else over me every time,
as I'm sure they'll finish the task at hand,
which is to say that whatever is in front of us
will get done if I'm not in charge of it.

There is a limit to the number of times
I can practice every single kind of mortification
(of the flesh?). I can turn toward you and say *yes,
it was you in the poem.* But when we met,

you were actually wearing a shirt, and the poem
wasn't about you or your indecipherable tattoo.
The poem is always about me, but that one time
I was in love with the memory of my twenties

so I was, for a moment, in love with you
because you remind me of an approaching
subway brushing hair off my face with
its hot breath. Darkness. And then light,

the exact goldness of dawn fingering
that brick wall out my bedroom window
on Smith Street mornings when I'd wake
next to godknowswho but always someone

who wasn't a mistake, because what kind
of mistakes are that twitchy and joyful
even if they're woven with a particular
thread of regret: the guy who used

my toothbrush without asking,
I walked to the end of a pier with him,
would have walked off anywhere with him
until one day we both landed in California

when I was still young, and going West
meant taking a laptop and some clothes
in a hatchback and learning about produce.
I can turn toward you, whoever you are,

and say you are my lover simply because
I say you are, and that is, I realize,
a tautology, but this is my poem. I claim
nothing other than what I write, and even that,

I'd leave by the wayside, since the only thing
to pack would be the candlesticks, and
even those are burned through, thoroughly
replaceable. Who am I kidding? I don't

own anything worth packing into anything.
We are cardboard boxes, you and I, stacked
nowhere near each other and humming
different tunes. It is too late to be writing this.

I am writing this to tell you something less
than neutral, which is to say I'm sorry.
It was never you. It was always you:
your unutterable name, this growl in my throat.

INTERROBANG

As an advocate for the precision of communication
I have to tell you that the typographically cumbersome

and unattractive combination of an exclamation
point sidled up to a question mark could be replaced

by a more compressed pairing; if the two separate
pieces of punctuation merge totally

into an outpouring of astonishment
to express modern life's incredibility—

Who forgot to put gas in the car‽
You call that a hat‽

Did you see the way she fell to her knees
in the supermarket because she was suddenly

overtaken by an erotic paranormal experience‽
—then faster breathing implies candor when we

shift these two elements together: I send
my love! You must carry yours in a luminous

tent rounded at the top? Latin for query
with a shout, in the dark I

seek you out as a witness because I adore
curiosity wrapped around wonder:

and in the second coming when I bare
my interrobang, located in the lower right corner

of nowhere you've seen, my skin does not tremble
before you, but rather

becomes punctuation for this illicit
almost-run-on sentence. My interrobang

should not be used in formal writing
as it's socially irresponsible and tangled

in knots over our inappropriate situation
which is exactly the shape of naked John Lennon

wrapped around clothed Yoko Ono, their
intertwined bodies (eternal, glorified) captured

just hours before he was shot—can you see
the way he clings to her as if he's drowning

in astonishment at his good luck?
John Lennon is dead and you and I—

you and I (‽) are separated by miles
of ticking, snarled night.

NIAGARA

Witness this: peonies and roses on the bedspread. Her red dress. The motel curtains sliding together to cover their view of parking lot oil stains and cigarette butts, the billboard that asks How Will The Falls Transform You? Their bodies give way, unresolved and stumbling. Afterwards, he stands in the rented doorframe listening to her shifting, her breath. In the half-melting drifts. In the creak of the car door before the slam. And how she breathes, like an accordion or a jewel box, and the sky opens. It's not the first time he prays for wonders instead of happiness. Cave of the Winds. Maid of the Mist. Rushing torrents of neon bouncing off the pavement between gaps in the motel curtains: aperture of plastic, chrome, electric light. Love is thrown and it is caught. It lives a long time in the air, floats on the surface of the skin. It can overflow, bounce like a fiddle string. It can be blurred, shaped like an onion peel. The half-moon of her body in this stained place, vertiginous. He hasn't written these words in a long time. He writes them with the motel pen. *If there was an apartment and I had a decent job and you felt happy and thought there could be a nice history together, would you come home?*

Past-Future/Future-Past

I tried to write you tonight
but there was nothing to say

If you already know the highway,
semis bearing down on asphalt

If you already know someone
who moans in their sleep

If you already know about crickets
or the wires of night stretching

like a fitted sheet, like a pencil compass
rounding the lines of the moon

and her consorts and are you in bed
with a counterpart and if so

then I am sure I already wrote you
about the train, its muffled whistle-

call insomnia, or the boxwoods,
twenty feet tall, reeking of decadence

and pilfered tradition
There's a phone booth here still

older than I am and I
was old enough to be used once,

and once, too, my stories
were not repeated, did not

repeat themselves in the phone booth
or to you when most nouns of this place

were unique and strange on my
tongue: farm, gravel, hay,

and scrap and dirt and
something singing

Terra Nullius

When we were done, all the buses had stopped running.
When we were done, the moon was painted large and
low-slung on the horizon. We sat like that a long time,
listening to each other exhale blue plumes of smoke
which tucked themselves through checkered screens.
It was near-morning and we were in our underwear.
It was near-dark and we were in our underwear,
my legs draped across his lap. Gentle curvature
of smoke—our bodies were looted, were broke.
Outside, invisible wires held up water towers and
busted street lamps. The sides of semis turned
the highway to gold threads. We had hallelujah
billboards. We had industrial rust. He put his finger
to my lips and I became the wreckage so we could find
our way back. We sat like that a long time.

Apologetics

A host of angels or a compass of cherubim
or maybe a resolution of sprites has absconded
with me or my common sense or possibly just
my best self and godknowswhatelse.

Which is to say I'm sorry.

I didn't mean to go to IHOP and spend the entire time
trying not to stare at the man in a reclining wheelchair
covered with a coverlet, sucking on oxygen
near the ladies' room.

I didn't mean to write you a letter that falls into
the oversharing category or scare you with Horace
or otherwise compromise what might have been
a perfectly fine correspondence (if not for my mention

of my copious tattoos or other youthful indiscretions).
I didn't mean to get a fever on this vacation, or yell at my son
in the bathroom of the BP station because he was touching
everything including the toilet seat. He always touches

the toilet seat in every bathroom. This is not new.
I did mean to go (which is to say I purposefully went)
to the aquarium and wondered how or why everyone else
seemed perfectly content with battling the crowds to see

otters or anemones. In the tank in The Pacific Reef exhibit
there was someone in an anonymous black scuba suit
standing and waving under the water; he/she was attached
to the window with a suction cup and gesticulated constantly,

mugged for pictures, fed the fish from a squirt bottle.
I learned *Beluga* is a Russian word. The Belugas were mating.

Or at least one named Beethoven was mating with another
whose name I don't remember because it wasn't a composer.

I started playing the violin when I was four—the same age
as my son. My teacher, Mrs. Eley, often cut my nails
with clippers she fished out from inside her piano.
My friend H. had the lesson after mine. He was

actually talented and some Fridays Mrs. Eley would ask him
to play whatever piece I struggled through so I could hear
how it was meant to sound, which was like the Long Island Sound
out her window at dusk—the beach being lapped by deep darkness;

the way the horsehair of a rosined bow, when pulled over strings,
smokes with small curls of dust. Years later, H. was killed
by a Metro-North train at the Riverdale station; the train's
engineer saw him jump from the platform.

I can hear the train here, though it doesn't matter where here is.
Everywhere is home for someone. This place has goats
and a rooster. When the bird went cockadoodledoo this afternoon
my son told him he could stop now since everyone was already up.

It is still night. Everyone is not already up.
The family is asleep and I'm typing this in the dark.
I once lived in a cottage with lemons in the front yard.
I once lived in a two-flat with a huge crape myrtle in the front yard.

I lived in many places that had no front yards at all.
The place I live in now has a dwarf cherry tree
that never recovered from one winter's frost.
I am telling you this because I have no common sense.

Retail Space Available

Because the image we make is painted
by flashlight: expired storefront, vacate
space where the elements didn't take
a toll on bits of smooth façade due to
signage: labelscar. Outskirts: because
our darks erase sirens in the distance,
pockmarked asphalt, the unknown
brightness of an indisposed place. Who
wraps us with compassion for the world
to come? The wilderness. Box elders
and couch grass crack through cement
block, return this refuge for cast-off
plastic shoes and discarded Chevys with
the squared-off trunks of three decades
ago to verdant. To once. Because we
rework time and space until both are
abandoned in a concrete grace: blown-
out sky, asperity, rippled bitumen,
monotonal hum. Because everything
beautiful is not far away. Because
one blue shopping cart knocked over,
joyridden, hears us sigh goodbye
twentieth century and the disposable
store glows quietly from within. In
the image of plenty we created them.
Because though this world is changing,
we will remain the same: abundant and
impossible to fill.

II

Maple Ridge

It rains and rains here. Steady.
In fits and starts. The rain bounces
off the screens like tentative bees,
like tacks pelted by an unseen hand.

We haven't left the house for forty days,
jokes Pastor Vince from his slick
deck next door. Every lawn
on the block has melded together,

grown to a meadow punctured
with delicate ecosystems of fungus
and calamity. The other neighbor's
boy runs through our yard

with a flower-shaped bruise
where his arm meets his chest.
His stepfather chases him down,
stops to show us a matched one

yellowing near his own shoulder—
recoil from the AK, he says proudly.
He was wantin to fire a 12-gauge shorty
at the range, but that woulda been

too much for him. Logan is
almost nine, so Give-Us-
Help-From-Trouble, O Lord,
Sunday's sermon at Pastor

Vince's congregation on bring-
your-weapon-to-church day:
"God, Guns, Gospel, & Geometry"
says the message board outside

Fieldstone, his parishioners packing
in the pews while we get on our knees
to tear out yellow networks of flowers
which outpace our violent efforts,

white and purple clover
that smell like wind and sugar
when they're beheaded by the mower.
We smooth things over

slowly. *Children! Don't rush.*
The month of May has arrived.
Now the rain is harder. The house
tears at its seams, vinyl-siding

stretching to accommodate
air, water, elemental gravities
that seep in while we sleep.
The wind does not howl.

It surgically disassembles
each set of metal chimes
we hang from the porch eaves.
It nods the tall grass

then tramples it like a pack
of roving dogs. Our small son
learned to open doors on his own
some time ago. When the rains stop.

When the rains never stop.
Somewhere a boy has a pistol
blazing a hole in his pocket
the size of the moon. The door

howls like the wind does not.
Somewhere a boy has an automatic

assault rifle. Flecks of rain
freckle his face. *Careful.*

The drops are not neutral.

and the moon   once it stopped   was sleeping

in the cold light   and the moon   while the wind snapped

vinyl siding apart   slipped around corners   whipped the neighbors'

carefully patterned   bunchgrass   our snow-filled   garden boxes

the house unjoining   the moon   our yard strips   covered

with hollow shells   hard remnants   ice   my son's breath

contiguous   static   shard   of green light

on the monitor   wavers   with coughs

the Baptist church   on Catawba   solitary   blazing

down the mountain   past midnight,   someone waving

their hands   at something   so quiet   you can hear

the wind tear   at the houses   you can hear   the neighbor

come home   though he's .18   acres away   it's too late

for that feeling   (possibility)   the night   always held

the wind   is at it   again   cracking paint

one day   it will   unroot us   one day

the wind   will tally   our losses

but not yet   the moon   not yet

Yizker Bukh

Memory is
flotsam (yes) just
below the surface
an eternal city
a heap of rubble
debris smaller
than your fist
an animal with-
out a leash
organized wreck-
age ghost net

or one hanging
silence on the phone—
she's gone, my sister said,
and we wept and wept
over my grandmother
while my sister sat
with her body and me
in the static and the rabbi
they sent told her to recite psalms
as comfort so we listened to each other
breathe instead and my sister's breath was
a tunnel a handful of pebbles a knotted
Chinese jump-rope   her breath was the coiled
terrycloth turban our grandmother wore when she cooked
or walked the shallow end of her condo pool for exercise—
our grandmother still somewhere in her white turban sewing
Cornish game hens together with needle and string or
somewhere in her good wig playing poker or
somewhere in her easy chair watching CNN
while cookies shaped like our initials bake
in her oven O memory how much you
erased how many holes   we punched

in your facts since who knows the stories
she never told about the camps there are
no marked graves just too much food on
holidays diabetes my mother's fear
of ships and the motion of some
suspension bridges O memory
you've left us trauma below
the surface and some above
like the fact that I can't
shake the December
my sister's red hair
caught fire from
leaning too close
to the menorah's
candles, our
grandmother
putting her
out with a
dish towel
with her
strong
arms.

AND THE MOON

shut in cold blue light,
in blown snow, my son's
static breath a forgiveness
a roadside x a since a wind-
shield a tunnel a handful
of pebbles.

Yiddishland

The people who sang to their children in Yiddish and worked in Yiddish
and made love in Yiddish are nearly all gone. Phantasmic. Heym.

Der may kumt shoyn on. The month of May has arrived. At the cemetery
my aunt has already draped my grandmother's half of the tombstone

with a white sheet. The fabric is tacked to the polished granite
by gray and brown rocks lifted from my grandfather's side of the plot.

He's been gone over twenty-five years. We are in Beth Israel Cemetery,
Block 50, Woodbridge, New Jersey for the unveiling and the sky is like lead.

We are in my grandmother's shtetl in Poland, but everyone is dead.
The Fraternal Order of Bendin-Sosnowicer Sick & Benevolent Society

has kept these plots faithfully next to their Holocaust memorial—
gray stone archway topped with a menorah and a curse: *Pour out Thy wrath*

upon the Nazis and the wicked Germans for they have destroyed the seed of Jacob.
May the almighty avenge their blood. Great is our sorrow, and no consolation is to be found!

My sister, in her cardboard kippah, opens her prayer book—a special edition
she borrowed from rabbinical school—and begins to read in Aramaic.

Not one of us can bring ourselves to add anything to the fixed liturgy.
My son is squatting at the next grave over, collecting decorative stones

from the Glickstein's double plot. We eat yellow sponge cake and drink
small cups of brandy to celebrate my grandmother's life. We are no longer mourners,

says Jewish law. Can we tell this story in Yiddish? Put the words in the right places?
My son cracks a plastic cup until it's shredded to strips, looks like a clear spider,

sounds like an error. When my sister finally pulls back the sheet, all the things
my grandmother was barely fit on the face of the marker. A year ago at the funeral,

her friend Goldie told me she was strong like steel, soft like butter—*women like that
they don't make any more.* My mother tries to show my grandmother—now this gray marker—

my son, how he's grown, but he squirms from her arms. *Ihr gvure iz nit tzu beshraiben.*
Her strength was beyond description. The people who sang to their children in Yiddish

and admonished them in Yiddish are nearly all gone, whole vanished towns that exist now
only in books, their maps drawn entirely by heart: this unknown continent, this language

of nowhere, these stones from a land that never was. *Der may kumt shoyn on.*
The month of May has arrived. *Der vind voyet.* The wind howls,

says I'm not a stranger anywhere. On the stones we write all we remember,
but we are poor guardians of memory. Can you say it in Yiddish? Can you bless us?

Inconsequential Alchemy

It's predictable summer again, the sun frosted and glaring like a cheap
Home Depot light fixture when it shines on the garden center

rife with landscaping plants that nobody loves but everyone buys as yard-filler:
pachysandra, rhododendron, euonymus, groundcover along with festive pansies

in black plastic six-packs that die by mid-July. There's no substitute for the figure
of a sunflower on a hill wilting past its stake, head drooped, body crucified.

The neighbor—the pastor's wife—tried to fill in the barren clay on the ridge
our houses share, but nothing thrives in this soil—not even the guaranteed

grass seed she bought that claims to grow on rock. But she's out watering anyway,
her chemo crew-cut glinting silver and ambiguous. Last season she offloaded

ziplocks of heirloom tulip bulbs from her freezer, told us to put them in our yard
since she was too weak to plant them. We buried them at the requisite depth

but they never came up; instead, a scourge of yellow trefoil entwined with the lawn.
This week she gives me three jars of home-preserved beets from their congregants.

Everyone must be praying for her, so that even those beets glow fuchsia on our counter,
countering the TV's ready-made alchemy. The local news is a strip-mall fire: remains

of an irreplaceable 1950s tricycle from the charred bike shop that had been in the family
for years. The form was recognizable, but the vehicle was literally a shadow

of itself, isometric charcoal, long and difficult. There are disruptions,
and there are disruptions. The news is always brought to us by Oakey's Funeral Home

& Crematory, and then on Sundays paid programming follows: Millennialist
news that trumpets the New World Order. Prophecies of the ages converging.

Specific details of the return, the eternal state of both the saved and the lost.
These exciting last days in which we live.

Snowpocalypse

Allegheny Mission, Big Spring Baptist, Community Christian Fellowship:
Saturday night news scrolls every church name in seven counties, services
more than postponed. We don't need the meteorologist to whisper *inclement*,
to warn us to stay indoors. We have a window shaped like a television set.

Tree lights flicker through a scrim of curtain next door where the pastor
of Fieldstone Christian and his wife plot their empty Sunday, sermon abandoned.
No one will hear anything about I am the holiness we are holy we pray for you
and maybe praise his name. The plow blinks yellow, scrapes the darkness,

shivers the drifts on our roofs, the hanging icicle lights. Inside, silence
wafts through the heating ducts. My son is asleep while the heavens
smudge from black to red. Snow sky. Hydrology. In the cul-de-sac,
there's nothing on except a few panes of the neighbor's window-glass

and some tilting FOR SALE signs. There's nothing on except the wind
pulling at our siding, clouds bruising the sky. The news says it was a snow TKO,
one for the history books, and in the morning, between storms, the neighbors shovel,
go out to buy bread. I set my son upright again in the high drifts in our yard.

I'm ok, he says each time I right him in his bib pants and boots. The pitch and yaw.
Convenience. We drive tenderly to the 7-Eleven. Milk. Maybe a newspaper.
Rock salt. He asks what convenience means. I don't have an answer.
I think holy. I think light. Later I tell him something about comfort. The news

drags in the evening, and with it, more snow. Our driveways retreat again
under the onslaught of white. We rest our weary feet on the ottoman, listen
to the neighbor's dog, who barks at the red sky then stops when she hears
the thin crescent moon wailing. There are truckers stuck on the interstate

who haven't eaten since yesterday. There are families sharing one thin blanket
on a high school floor. The news says stay in your vehicle, don't wander and get
frostbitten, don't spin your wheels—you'll only dig in deeper. We are glowing
with televised radiance so nothing can hurt us. The news says *this is an ongoing situation.*

To Whom It May Concern:

Please excuse me from the meeting.
I'm feeling small and non-combative.

It's below freezing, so we have no daycare.
The cable box is broken. The satellite

is misaligned. To Whom It May Concern:
The salt on the road crunches like teeth

so I can't make the meeting because
I am using my fingernail to rub

a critical note into the ice
on the neighbor's mailbox.

My tires are spinning in ellipses.
To Whom It May Concern:

My acupuncturist says my Qi
is puny, and the last time we met

someone told me to shut the fuck up.
I hate your monogrammed dress cuffs

so please conduct the meeting
without me as I'm suffering

from zipper failure. I'm hopped up
on caffeine and twitching. I'm battery

operated and recalcitrant. To Whom
It May Concern: I'd rather be reading

the story about the elephant crouching
in the corner trying not to be noticed

by the zookeeper's wife in her ruffled
sleep cap to my son. I'd rather be reading

the book to him where the snowman
actually dies in the end. To Whom

It May Concern: I understand
the task is important, but I do not

want to be part of this committee.
I've been buried by ribbons of snow

in a giant frozen dazzling. The universe
is changing to a white cereal bowl

with lots of rivets and I've been told
we live on the frost line. Please excuse me

from this meeting. Dark energy is shoving
the cosmos apart and it's best explored

in the pure environment of Antarctica.
To Whom It May Concern: I've moved

to the most difficult place on earth.
It's impossibly blue and blazing.

One Version of December

There's something about the ice today that reminds me of the plastic kerchief my grandmother would wear over her wig and tied under her chin on days it rained, her synthetic hair the texture of spun sugar on a paper cone, a shade lighter than dirt under that translucent tarp. The ice skates across asphalt, deck-wood, slicks railings, shines sideways and crackles. It reaches its sharp hands into the dirt to root. The blank styrofoam head and neck where her wig rested sits empty on her dresser. A lifetime ago there were chickens in someone's front yard, and my grandmother watched over me. *You will be blessed*, she always implied, with her hands. It is winter and I return there. Sad girl with an unyielding triangle. Sad girl with a styrofoam head. Sad girl with nostalgia. We leave our attachments in a landscape (deeply felt, uneventful). The eternal city is not the hereafter but a cheap plastic copy with a crocheted ocean wrapped in blandness and littered with shiny cars. My grandmother's styrofoam head ripples with laughter and confusion, my grandmother in her white sun hat, her white turban, the ever more ancient man she hired annually in his white captain's hat to pick my sister and I up from the Fort Lauderdale airport in his Lincoln Continental. The one time I tried to drive myself in a rental I got so lost I had to stop at the Lucky Boy Motel for directions. It was night. There was bulletproof glass and the Vacancy signs lining US-1 shined pink, turquoise, the colors most opposite of ice. Her eyeless head, her head that would float on the Intracoastal, bob like a buoy then get swept out to sea, that won't nod anymore as if she were listening to us complain about the sun, the heat, "Feliz Navidad" playing on the slow drive from the airport each December, our faces tilted to the windshield.

Wal★Mart Supercenter

God Bless America says the bumper sticker on the racer-red
Rascal scooter that accidentally cuts me off in the Walmart parking lot
after a guy in a tricked-out jeep with rims like chrome pinwheels tries
to pick me up by honking, all before I make it past the automatic doors
waiting to accept my unwashed hair, my flip-flops, my lounge pants.

The old man on the scooter waves, sports a straw boater banded in blue & white,
and may or may not be the official greeter, but everyone here sure is friendly—
even the faces of plastic bags, which wink yellow and crinkle with kindness,
sound like applause when they brush the legs of shoppers carrying them
to their cars. In Port Charlotte, a woman's body was found in a Jetta

in a Walmart parking lot. In a Walmart parking lot in Springfield,
a macaque monkey named Charlie attacked an eight-year-old girl.
I am a Walmart shopper, a tract-house dweller—the developments
you can see clearly from every highway in America that's not jammed up
on farmland or pinned in by mountains. I park my car at a slant in the lot,

hugged tight by my neighbors' pickups. I drive my enormous cart
through the aisles and fill it with Pampers, tube socks, juice boxes, fruit.
In the parking lot of the McAllen Walmart, a woman tried to sell six
Bengal tiger cubs to a group of Mexican day laborers. A man carjacked
a woman in the parking lot of the West Mifflin Walmart, then ran

under a bridge and disappeared. Which is to say that the world
we expect to see looks hewn from wood, is maybe two lanes wide,
has readily identifiable produce, and the one we've got has jackknifed itself
on the side of the interstate and keeps skidding. The one we've got has clouds
traveling so fast across the sky it's like they're tied to an electric current.

But electricity is the same for everybody. It comes in the top of your head
and goes out your shoes, which will walk through these automatic doors.
In the Corbin Walmart parking lot a woman with a small amount of cash

was arrested for getting in and out of trucks. A man stepped out of his car
in the Columbus Walmart parking lot, and shot himself. I get in the checkout line

behind a lighted number on a pole. The man in front of me jangles coins
in his pocket, rocks back and forth on his heels. The girl in front of him
carefully peels four moist dimes from her palm to pay for a small container
of honey-mustard dipping sauce. In the parking lot of the LaFayette Walmart,
grandparents left their disabled two-year-old grandson sitting in a shopping cart

and drove away. Employees in the parking lot at the La Grange Walmart
found a box containing seven abandoned kittens. I am not a Christian or
prone to idioms, but when the cashier says she is grateful for small mercies,
I nod in assent. *Kyrie eleison, Christe eleison.* The Latin root of mercy
means price paid, wages, merchandise, though now we use it as

compassion shown to a person in a position of powerlessness,
and sometimes forgiveness towards a person with no right
to claim it. God is merciful and gracious, but not just.
In the Walmart parking lot in Stockton, a man considered armed
and dangerous attacked his wife, beating her unconscious.

A couple tried to sell their six-month-old for twenty-five bucks
to buy meth in the Salinas Walmart parking lot. We who are in danger,
remember: mercy has a human heart. Mercy with her tender mitigations,
slow to anger and great in loving-kindness, with her blue employee's smock
emblazoned with *How may I help you?* Someone in this place have mercy on us.

You return the Torah to the ark

and I think of the distant past
eins tsvey dray fir now thirty years
since I was a child and used to count
men's hats in my grandparents'

synagogue the moment everyone
rose up but not the ladies—
they stood and I didn't count them
finf zeks zibn akht as instead of hats

they wore latticed doilies
pinned to their wigs, scraps
of lace flat as an outstretched hand
conferring a webbed blessing

or folded like wings about
to take flight *nayn tsen elf tsvelf*
before whom did we stand?
the male Rabbi, the male Cantor

and his *oyoyoys draytsn fertsn*
fuftsn zekhtsn the ark shuts
in a flash of white an arm
crossing the heart the chest

a house for the body is rending
of garments—a curtain's pull
zibetsn akhtsn nayntsn tsvantsik
Zichron Moshe, Adath Israel,

Ward Avenue Shul and who knows
what shteebles are demolished are
churches now this second post-war
shtetl of ladies and gentlemen the Bronx

is burning is burned the congregation
sighs into their seats and I think of
cousin Freddy's story about the Rabbi
(name long forgotten) who would call out

Yankees scores during high holiday
davening *ein un tsvantsik tsvey un tsvantsik*
everyone could hear the ballpark crowd
cheering through the open doors

The Architecture of Memory

Dear yellow backhoe, dear yellow grader, dear yellow bulldozer:
you decipher and dismember our dirt, clay red from iron oxide,

topsoil stripped by development. How did anyone bury their dead
here, when no spot yields to a shovel? Down the block

I've seen tiny walled-off clusters of headstones for families who sold
their farmland to make our tract homes, but it's like chipping away

at stone to get past the first façade of our yard which cracks like
earthquake cement, holds water like a sealed basin. My son

loves to curl his hands into half moons and press them together
as a bowl, flatten them to a book. I've been reading the *sefer zikoren*,

the *yizker-bikher* that recount how survivors like my grandmother
searched their hometowns in vain after the war for familiar bones

to bury, and then for their peacetime dead, only to find the streets
paved with Hebrew inscriptions, gravestones face-up. Avenging ghosts.

Maybe you're already there, grandmother, bulldozer. Rendered.
Surfaced with asphalt. The iron gate to the entrance where the cemetery

once stood.

Each morning in the car my son yells, *Detour!*, reminds me we're taking
the new way since the road is broken. Orange yield sign, orange cone,

exhumed coffin of the soon-to-be playground, the promised pool;
heaps of gravel grow and vanish in minutes, and O the brick piles,

the retaining walls that fit (dip-click) into each other. I will crochet
my son an afghan of a dump truck, of a backhoe, of a crane

like the one we stopped to watch this week outside school
raising large metal pipes high above the stadium. We held hands

and looked past the chain-link fence papered in green mesh
like a present, past the see-saw and drying sandbox. Dear

bulldozer, dear grandmother, we are placeless. We are placeful
but unrooted. We are boomburbs and copia. We are excavated

and hoisted. We are rubble. We are

all new and renovated, and when we go in that rapture
the neighbor preaches on each Sunday (rupture past memory perished)

there will be no ashes. We will be caught up together above
alleyways stoops fire-escapes storefronts—all the things

we don't have in our subdivision, all the things that shined
in your Bronx, from the window of the Grand Concourse apartment—

and before the traffic and rooftops crumble we will ascend in clouds
of dirt and steel and smoke that spell out warnings: Do not stay here long.

Leave as quickly as you can once you have fulfilled the mitzvah,
as it is written: obligation : locate   obligation : procreate.

Dear grandmother, these are for the most part words not gravestones,
gravestones not books to ward off the melancholy of dusk, a paper cemetery

sited next to an arterial cluster of what? To carry out the commandment
to remember and remember and then bury it.

LET THE FUTURE BEGIN THIS WAY:

a house goes up & says Amen
then falls down

which means whole neighborhoods
fade away like that,

with one holy blessing
in the distressed light

ground to gravel,
sputtering engines

of grit & shingle
& shunned dust.

Dust!
The blind angel

of Detroit: head
like a bullet, dollar sign

for a heart. Time was
when even the Bronx

put cheery faces
on crumbling façades:

bright plastic decals
with shutters, curtains,

flowerpots, and even
occupants—what could it hurt?

The old neighborhood was verdant
but not magical, bombed out

but not foolhardy;
go by, and even

thirty years later
the same neighbor

still sits on the stoop.
Let that gutted truth

carry our bodies safe
[between the railway lines] safe

to the shores
of prosperity

where American ruins
stand for failure,

drag us down: things
used to be better;

now, someone
in every city

is guilty
of anonymous assemblages—

heaps of discarded
objects to help us

unforget neighbors
who should have faded

(I watched you disappear
once)

How long? Not long—
How long? Not long—

I feel deeply
that this comfortable existence

How long?
Not long—

is transitory—
that my real home is

How long?
Not long—

in some form
of ghetto,

for whosoever shall call
upon crumbling façades

shall be saved
(from what?)

though the little world
between the railway lines

. . .
has (long) been swept away

How long?
Not long—

Bleak beauty, good friend
gone blind, can't you see

the neighborhood
smashed to brick dust?

How beautiful
are the feet

of those who bring
good news of good things.

Maple Ridge

It is nearly Halloween, which means
wrong sizes on Walmart racks, variety bags of
        pumpkins extinguishing themselves on the stoop

children from the trailer park trawling our identical lawns soon
so we can give away nickels, light, sandpaper, raisins, cement.

But the wind comes first and takes the neighbor's
        airbrushed Honda   porch couch   dead flowers.

The wind comes and peels the neighbor's shingles,
        flaps the shades, bends their yard-weeds.

The wind comes and
                drives the main drag restlessly
        looking for
trauma and muscle cars.

The wind comes as a small sacrifice
        to the gods of disconsolation.
Their innards will burn.

It is nearly Halloween and we've hollowed
        the bent windows, smoothed over the unlit windows

but we can't do anything about the last
        of the neighbor's cigarette. When he walks
                smoke parachutes
        in the space between   our houses:
                a tattooed Iraq war vet,
        and his nightly   light pollution.

We can count on the neighbor's cigarette,
and children flock to our street, sweet things.

We don't turn anyone away.

III

The Book of Dissolution

Because it is an uninhabited place, because it makes me hollow, I pried open the pages of Detroit: the houses blanked out, factories absorbed back into ghetto palms and scrub-oak, piles of tires, heaps of cement block. Vines knock and enter through shattered drop-ceilings, glassless windows. Ragwort cracks the street's asphalt to unsolvable puzzles. What lives upon its own substance and dies when it devours itself? The question shrinks and sticks between my ribs with toughness. The plaster flowers I collect in my pocket don't travel well, crumble to dust. Even the rigid balustrades splinter and cave in. What shall come to pass? Chaos of lathe and plaster, baseboards and mold. The wood that framed rooms is bulldozed is cited is picked clean is abandoned is a prairie where a neighborhood once stood. Fire is a force for good in this place; the later it is put out the better; there will always be something left over. Trees grow thirty feet up through a gaping hole left by skylights collapsed in the heat of flames. Burn scars on cement where scrappers torched the last bits of plastic off copper wire spell out code that reveals what the world will look like when we're gone. I have been unoccupied I have been foreclosed I have been vacant for a long time. Everything of any real value has been looted: my pulse, my breath, my hereafter. The most intimate place of all in this city of sadness is the distance between sounds: testifying pheasants and wild dogs, amens of saws, amens of sledgehammers. I am a house waiting to fall in on itself or burn while a homeless man walks down the middle of the street pushing a baby stroller full of sheet metal ductwork. An enclosure is the most difficult thing to steal so I'll follow him and then I'll know where to go from here.

POST-INDUSTRIALIZATION

This is the single greatest story of American success:
God Bless Our Customers. Fax & Copy Here. Beer
& Wine & Liquor. Gifts & Perfumes & Lottery & Cell.

Check Cashing & Quick Weaves. I saw signs and wonders,
wonders and signs, but no one lugged me from the rubble
with an outstretched hand. I did not rise from the ashes.

In 1914, Henry Ford offered five dollars a day to the men
who assembled the Model T. And the dead were judged
according to their works. What kind of people

could walk away from something like this?
All of us. We like space, we like cars. A city
in decay releases energy: rebar, sirens, razor-

wire, spray paint, a guy pushing a shopping cart
down 2nd Street with a vacuum cleaner in it. Destroy
what destroys you. Then, from the ruins, Hallelujah.

This is happening all over the country. Detroit as cipher
of decay: mirror mirror. And I saw the dead, small and great,
stand before the city. Their fate was tagged on slabs

of plaster with Krylon. And the devil that deceived them
was cast into the lake of fire. And the books were opened.
And the books were burned. *What must I do to be saved?*

Photograph the bricks peeling slowly off the rear
of the Wurlitzer Building, threatening an alley
where a squatter hangs one pair of shorts

and one shirt on a makeshift clothesline tied
to a busted fire-escape running along a wall
which has a single red heart painted in every

cracked window. Those Wurlitzer organs
had such lifelike power that they made people
who never sang when they were alone

join in chorus with others. This is where
we start: with great terror,
with miraculous signs and wonders.

By Other Means

My body as terra nullius. My body as celestial. My body as dysfunctional. This water-damaged waiting room. This explicable flood of couples with expectant grins. The grim single-mother with hair past her waist and plastic Dollar Tree bag as purse. The girl in the hallway asking about my hair, diamond studs on either side of her lip pinning her smile. This exam table. This white sheet below my waist. This white sheet reeking of bleach. Your wisecracking Resident. Your overly-friendly Resident. Your Resident making me anonymous. Your Resident making me ashamed. I will show you, Resident, the one corner of Detroit where the houses love me, my sheen, since I am as cavernous, as broke-down. Where the houses don't talk back or ask how the procedure went. The vast territory of my ovaries on screen, their black holes, their stellar mass. The whole solar system is bursting, splintering, flaring, and I am not. Planets spin on their axes and people are launched into space. I am the territory no one will inhabit. The borderlands of *motherhood* and *not again*. Want has no business here.

Ghostbox

The first time we went, we forgot
a flashlight. This was outside
Detroit so there was ample
parking. Acres of steel arms
that herded shopping carts in
for pep talks—their rails stood
quiet, parallel, signaling the end
of the diaspora. Never mind
the under-performing automatic
doors. They surrendered first,
hugged themselves shut. We
went back and stood on the roof
of a car to watch the building
smolder. In one account, we
heard gun-shots but didn't
drive off. In another, we met a
coyote, and a red fox when the
sun came up. There was ample
parking. It's worth repeating.
And the distance. The distance
was unrazed, dusted, fenced,
tagged, shuttered. The distance,
most of all, was unlit.

In/exhaustible

Martinsville, VA

The billboards into town advertise Southern Gun
& Pawn, Slot Cars, say Everyone's Preapproved!
Best Deal on a Home, Period—the prefabs that come

in halves on the back of trucks labeled WIDE LOAD,
and this was a manufacturing town, until the factories
closed up shop, the warehouses turned to churches

with food pantries, roadways littered with signs:
Are Your Bills Crippling You? Psalm 75:1. Ferguson
Tire: We Buy Gold, then Welcome to Martinsville—

A City Without Limits says the sign on the road in,
and there behind the rows of shotgun houses, a dye plant,
abandoned, two mottled smokestacks rising like goalposts,

no longer pumping out anything of worth near the sign
that says Bankruptcy Could Be Your Solution (All Welcome),
the sign that says We Love You Pastor. Get Well Soon.

The sign says Cash for Old Broken Jewelry, and this
is a town where everyone's broke or gone. It is
Christmastime in Martinsville, and Santa in his red robes,

in his Shriner's hat, stands regal and fat in the darkened
consignment store. Molded sheep rest on cotton batting
near a nest made from hay. The faded wise men kneel

with hands clasped, gazing at that baby with outstretched arms.
In another window, lit-up swaying snowmen share a hymnal,
and the plastic baby rests among doves, nestled by a lady

in blue robes with her head bowed. This is a city
of supplication, of duct-taped and empty storefronts,
of faded holiday ornaments, where downtown businesses

only open three days a week—a city that left its smokestacks
raised in prayer to the signs, and the sign says Highest Prices
Paid in Cash, says HUGE Furniture & Mattress Sale.

Some billboards quote a politician: "Attracting New Jobs"
but the local radio talk show has callers buzzing, all asking
the same question: *when is our train gonna come in when*

is our train comin in where is that train and can you hear it
in the peeling storefronts, the empty storage facilities,
the degree completion joints? The walk-ins welcome,

the spider-webbed glass, the abandoned call centers?
People speak of your wonderful deeds. The plastic families
wear wire halos, and fold their arms to wait and wait.

Someone will bring work. The smokestacks
are out of breath. The sign at Lays It Away
says Happy Thanksgiving to All and God Bless.

ALL THAT BLUE FIRE

Alvin Brewer, former Ford autoworker (Detroit, MI)

I'm from Virginia. Gasburg, Virginia.
And I heard that the plants were hiring,

so what I did, I came up here
for a New Year's party.

And after I went to the New Year's party,
I didn't ever go back.

I went to the Ford Motor Company
because they were hiring. That was
the 3rd of January, 1969.

My first job was working in the engine plant,
where they build the motors at.

I just came up here to a New Year's party
and got this job and never go back.

They have the motors hanging on a line,
and they'd be passing through,
so one guy turns the crank,

one guy put a piston in,
then you turn the crank again,
and another guy put a piston in.

Yeah, they go on down the line
like that. Then when it get out
to another part of the line,

they lay the motor down,
they put the heads on,
spark plugs in.

And then it gone on out—
they turn the motor over,

put the oil pan on,
keep on down the line.

When the motor get to the back,
they be ready to start it up.

They hook up the hoses
and the gas line, start it up

right there, less than half an hour.
When I would go on break, sometimes

I would go back there, watch them guys
hook the hoses up and start em up,
cause I used to like to hear them started up.

All that blue fire be shooting out of there
when the motor first started, cause they

ain't got no pipes on it.
Sound real loud, that blue fire
from the exhaust system.

Once they put that carburetor on there,
they just pour the gas, hook the gas line up,
hit the accelerator a couple of times,

and there you go. Start right up.
They started it without the body.
The engine don't be in the body yet.

I just came up here to a New Year's party
and got this job and never go back.

Man they were having so much fun.
Back then, I didn't want to go back.

Outside the Abandoned Packard Plant

closed fifty-four years, the crickets
are like summer, are like night

in a field, but it is daytime. It is August.
There is no pastoral in sight—only

Albert Kahn's stripped factory, acres
of busted and trembling brick façade

so vast there must be thousands
of crickets rubbing their wings

beneath makeshift thresholds of PVC
piping tangled in ghetto palm saplings

growing through a deflated mattress top
tossed over rusted industrial metal the shape

of an elephant dropped on its knees
dispensing invisible passengers into

moats of rubble dappled with what?
These crickets, their industrious wings

mimicking silence and song, lonely
background, until one beat-up maroon

Buick flies down Concord, accelerating
like the road just keeps going, like he'll

actually get away with whatever he's doing,
then two white cop cars, Doppler sirens

shrieking and braiding, but it is peaceful
other than that—you might think

you're in the country as in not the city
as in wilderness under the bridge that used to say

MOTOR CITY INDUSTRIAL PARK
and now just punched out eyes and ARK

And After the Ark

The Heidelberg Project, 3600 Block of Heidelberg Street (Detroit, MI)

what was left behind was astounding:

dead trees wearing upside-down shopping carts on their hands
conference call phones, black and ringless, resting on a park bench
a pile of singleton shoes crowned with a blue plastic dump truck
and the signs: Camel Cigarettes Pleasure to Burn $ Special Offer
Toasted Double Melts, 2 for $4, and Yahweh scrawled everywhere

WHY WAS THE ARK AND FLOOD NECESSARY?
Because no one was able to catch a taxi out of Detroit.
They were only, it turns out, cardboard cutouts.
(take you in a taxi—God can taxi you to New York
        taxi   taxi)

WHAT DOES THE ARK LOOK LIKE?
See: America's Greatest Manufacturing Experience
See: Perfect Industrial Complex
See: horsepower, engine block
See: symbol of the American spirit

WHAT ANIMALS WERE TO BE LOADED ON BOARD?
I can't tell you that. I can only describe the creatures
(all stuffed) that were abandoned—plush lambs, a bunny,
a giant floppy dog, something that might have been
a mouse, possibly a pig, but mostly teddy bears
nailed to porch stairs or rotting siding, deflated
and torn by the wind, uncolored by the rain until
all the animals belong to the same (god)forsaken clan.

And You Shall Say God Did It

but really it was racism/poverty/economics/inequality/violence/
deindustrialization/cars/suburbia/mismanagement/corruption

and all the factories of the great city burst apart
and the floodgates of the sky broke open
and schools and jobs were blotted out
but day and night did not cease

and all the flesh that stirred in the city persisted

the buildings held their ground and used trees
to anchor themselves to the land

and O Yahweh, the sunflowers—have you seen
the tangle of sunflowers in the yard?

THE LANGUAGE OF HAPPINESS

is not present if there has been a change of partners
(there has been no change of partners)

is the house with a notice taped to the door
& abandoned glow-in-the-dark stars still adhered
to the foreclosed ceiling & the developer

says it will never sell—the basement has been
condemned, did you see the exposed rebar?

The language of happiness
is an inherently inwardly focused experience
is a private affair
is the new black

because my mother went
to the shrouded grave of the Rebbe
& Jesus loves my body like

an empty plastic egg that breaks
in half at the waist waiting to be filled
with small gifts (if we were lying

we'd clap our mouths) I'm just
not telling you everything
youbetterbelieve & blessyourheart

is always stressful,
this language of happiness
is wrecking our friendship
(you're pregnant)

is hectic: I drive the highway
& drive the highway & drive

the highway—you get the picture—
& wait for a woman to say my name
in the waiting room of the language

of happiness we are engaged in collusion
to solve a common problem that is often
quickly treatable, a condition of the [inexplicable]
that impairs conception

the language of happiness is not bracketed—
three unprotected years of nature & then some
for a common problem, a system, an inability
despite an act of love strongly associated
with a body, dear body, can you be

a speeding cab that stops to pick up
a passenger, even if you're off duty?
The driver is on his cell phone again.

We're on the West Side Highway, body,
& behind those lit windows people
are folding & folding & folding
themselves in half like paper.
O fortune teller. O future.

Inside the Frame

a man leans in the doorway of his not-home
waiting to be photographed from a passing car

by a man who is dreaming of trespassing
and resurrecting the last bricks

from every demolished school [dwelling] church
he ever entered or abandoned himself in/to

before he left Detroit/this city

Rivera painted an infant huddled
in the bulb of a plant, a mother

hoarding apples in her circled arms
a harvest, a plenty
Jewelry * Loans * Cash Fast—

a billboard with a diamond
ring for every finger
and on the walls, so many hands

working the line/turning the cranks
(holy rollers) grasping rocks
~~while we look on~~

it don't exist, says the plywood
door (attended to, cracked open)
at Bill's Blue Star Disco Lounge,

burned down so the sky shines
through the not-roof on/to Michigan Avenue
the whole road gap-toothed, boarded up

and then Woodward, where the parking
attendant swears he'll stay ~~outside the frame~~
in the lot with the cars till the game lets out

OUTSIDE THE FRAME

is a brand new $115 million dollar high school with the same name as the abandoned one outside the frame are two men biking at midnight down John R street with red lights blinking off their cycles like Morse code it's not too dangerous outside the frame are the lines around Michigan Avenue for Slows Bar B Q outside the frame are the larger contexts for these shots the what's next and what's next to the slots of abandoned tagged houses and houses that went so long ago that only field is left not even foundations those have grown over with prairie grass did you see the pheasants outside the frame is a functioning farm an urban garden where one horse neighs in the heat nuzzles the dirt outside the frame stands a blue sign with two yellow suns and Hope Takes Root outside the frame is the Obama gas station at the intersection of Plymouth and Wyoming with rebranded awnings & signs & pumps and outside the frame the owner says I have my dream and my dream came true outside the frame is the possibility to do whatever the hell you want no one cares what we do here outside the frame is the blues jam at the corner of Frederick and St. Aubin so bring your lawn chairs to the abandoned lot where they pass the hat for the mowing Porta-Potties electric generator to run the amps because outside the frame sometimes there's just nobody around to say you can't

Borderama

Inside me is a playground, is a factory.
Inside me is a cipher of decay.
I am sometimes a vehicle for absorbing wealth.
I feel daily like I have to defend myself.
Inside me is inbred chaos.
Inside me is America's greatest manufacturing experience.
Inside me is an assembly line four miles long
where the workers who build products
are themselves interchangeable parts.
Inside me is a big blue Cadillac.
Inside me is a shrunken footprint.
Inside me are things that are not relevant
to anyone's idea of a civilization in ruins—
a moment of consolation, a transitory
slideshow, a centerfold.

Inside me is someone saying we will
rebuild this city. Inside me is the legacy
of tanks rolling down the Boulevard,
an arsenal of scrapped schools
with graffiti on the doors—
I'm Alone ♥
I have Lost
my ♥ children.
Skys Tha Limit.
Inside me I've got
a window
where my heart is

but we hope for better things.
If we don't act so bad, they won't close the school.
If you close the school, there's nothing here.
Inside me is the fate of a neighborhood.
And something hard that refuses to die.

Is that plywood torn off?
Can I fit through that hole?
Inside me they've left everything behind:
maps, test tubes, disintegrating plaster,
bent rebar, torn conveyor belts
where three guys worked the engine
and one guy turned the crank.
I was an autoworker for 33 years,
she said, *and you learn your job so well*
that it looks like you're part of the line,
it looks like you're dancing, like the guy alone
on John R Street outside his black sedan—
August night and his car doors open,
music pouring out, doing a graceful
running man. I want to tell him
about the lost colony, the people
that landed and vanished inside me.
And this photographer I talked to
on the phone who thinks Detroit
is still on her way down, hasn't hit
bottom. But there's Harmonica Shah
in his overalls in a lot on the corner
of Frederick and St. Aubin singing
if you don't like the blues, you got a hole
in your soul. If you don't like the blues,
go home.

Terra Nullius

The poem in which we drive an hour to the beach and Uncle Dave doesn't get out of his lawn chair once.

The poem in which we left the yellow plastic shovel behind and everyone is bereft.

The poem in which I can't stop talking about how you walked deep into Lake Erie and the water was still only up to your knees when you turned into a speck past the rock jetty.

The poem in which everyone listens to celebrity gossip in the car on the way back.

The poem in which I pontificate on how ugly the fiancée of that Jonas brother is, and how they're too young to get married, and how my grandmother's old neighbor would have said, "Ugly? She can't help that she's ugly. It's that she's so stupid," and I would have yelled at her for assuming that all former hairdressers are dim.

The poem in which I turn into my grandmother's old neighbor.

The poem in which I remember very clearly how they both stored tissues in their bras.

The poem in which I think about how this would horrify your mother—the pendulous breasts, the moist tissues, the dipping into the cleavage to retrieve anything.

The poem in which your mother tries not to wince when I order whatever I want from the menu despite her coupon for two medium 1-topping pizzas.

The poem in which I try to find a deeper meaning for why I notice the woman ahead of us in line at Johnny's Liquor Store who buys a pack of menthols and asks the guy behind the counter if he knows her good-for-nothing brother. She has hair that looks like cats got at a skein of yarn, and a tattoo above her ankle that's dark and unspecified. It's far enough above her ankle that it's nearly mid-calf—like her ankle and calf are two different countries and the tattoo got lost in the borderlands on the way to its actual destination.

The poem in which I am territory that is under dispute and no one will occupy it because of fear and uncertainty.

The poem in which I reach the conclusion that this feeling is inspired by your mother and the way she hums out-of-season carols while doing kitchen tasks, though it's not really about the humming but rather the time she asked me to light the Hanukkah candles in the attic because it would be better if they were out of the way for the Christmas party.

The poem in which you and I are in line waiting to buy a mixed six-pack of Great Lakes and I am staring at a stranger's tattoo and thinking about the fact that I am not Anne Frank while the baby is in the car with your mother.

The poem in which I go into Walmart and buy the baby an olive-green cap that looks suspiciously like Fidel Castro's.

The poem in which I could eradicate the fact that I ever went into Walmart and bought anything so the baby can one day start a revolution.

The poem in which we see a couple on the highway median in a stalled-out Buick and don't stop to help.

The poem in which the highway median looks like the spit of land between two enemy trenches and I feel a deep longing for my childhood.

The poem in which I remember, for no apparent reason, the tornado instructions taped to the sides of all the filing cabinets in one office I worked in that was on the top floor of a mostly abandoned mall in Overland Park, Kansas. All that was left: decorative fountains, floor tiles, mirrored ceilings, Nearly Famous Pizza, the carcass of Sears.

The poem in which we leave Northeastern Ohio. The poem in which we return to Northeastern Ohio.

The poem in which it is night and we are lost in Northeastern Ohio and we keep passing Amish buggies adorned with reflective tape.

The poem in which the moon is a vehicle for content, and is far less than a perfect reflector of anything.

The poem in which we are all in some kind of limbo.

Cosmogony/Progeny

Here there is no lasting city;
instead, an immense field
of vision which is not necessarily
hazy, but filled with structures
that begin to list and spit brick
& gutters & vinyl siding &

we cannot remain standing
in this apocryphal landscape
where or when there is still
the possibility of a miracle
happening in the form of
signs & wonders, wonders

& signs: CheckCashing or
WorkWear or BeautyMart.
But we remain standing.
So rise up, whoever you are,
the last hope for this place
where unused billboards

proffer see-through clues
to the future. To drive
along the highway is to
see life with its unanswered
questions and structures
of want. Rise up,

tract houses. Fall in line
and march to the sounds
of a thousand backhoes
beeping in reverse, prophesying
omygod & *comeholyspirit*,
singing of everything they've

taken away and razed over.
Remember: I still believe
we will find you in the rubble
of the city, in the cast-off stones
lining this place. And when
Hannah wept she was not drunk,

though some days I am drunk
and do not weep, and some days
I weep and do not drink.
I don't often pray, blessmyheart,
but if I did, I would veer
from fixed liturgy and speak

in tongues about how much love
I've plowed under waiting
for you. One day I will crouch
anywhere but in a pew
and tell you that most
origins are mysterious

while simultaneously
combing the crowd
for some signal or
synchronicity.
The truth is
even cities

are ephemeral
(Say farewell!)
& woe to us
if we reject
that rule.
The truth is

I'm quick
to bow down
at the altars
of anyone's wild
& imperfect feet.

ARS POETICA WITH RADIO APPARATUS, TODDLER, & DUCKS

A local convention of ham radio operators
at the duck pond's gazebo have erected towers
to try to bounce their signals off the moon.

My son thinks their metal scaffolding
is the Eiffel Tower—thinks all metal towers
are the Eiffel Tower ever since we read him

that book which features a world-traveling pig.
We have come to feed the ducks stale potato buns.
Every time my son tosses a hunk he is mobbed

by ducks whose feathers glint in the light.
They both terrify and delight him. Each duck
has an electric blue racing stripe, a wing-feather

the color of a vintage GTO. Pontiac may have
gone under, but the ham radio operators tout
survivability with their giant portable antennae.

"We can jury-rig something on any spot,"
one guy in a fishing hat tells me, and this
earth-moon-earth communicating

happening just for today is apparently
the equivalent of climbing Mount Everest
when it comes to radiograms since the moon

is a poor sounding board—since the moon
is spinning and has a rough surface that disrupts
signals. I try to explain to my son that these men

are talking through the air, but I forget
that he doesn't know about air. He knows
about outer space and understands

that we live on earth and that the Eiffel Tower
has something, now, to do with the ducks
and the moon. But how to explain an element

that's invisible, that surrounds us, that covers
the earth like an orange peel and keeps us alive?
There is no wind so I tell him to spin around

and listen. But what he hears, I know, instead
of the swish of air shushing around his ears
is a motley Doppler effect: ducks honking

and the clang of these radio buffs
tinkering with a rusting web of metal, murmuring
to unseen strangers who only know them

by their handles, their call signs, each letter made clear
with a noun—Victor Whiskey X-ray Papa Foxtrot Echo—
who, for today only, are letting passersby try out

their equipment, send and accept real messages,
like ONE (everyone safe here—please don't worry),
or TWO (coming home as soon as possible).

These voices spilling into space, reflecting radio
waves off the aurora borealis, off ionized trails
of meteors, waiting for someone to pluck them
from the darkness, decipher their code.

Porto, Portare, Portavi, Portatus

At the airport the conveyor bears small yachts shaped like luggage
into the distance, and I am headed, when they let me pass

through the x-ray arch, toward home. There is a distance
sometimes greater than this between us, since you are in

another state—gaseous, solid, liquid, light—and I admit
I am often absent lately from whatever is happening

in a given room. Portatus. Having been carried from one place
to another, I will be delayed in this terminal in Akron, Ohio

for the longest dusk, but I do not yet know this. I spend hours
trying to puzzle out the black script running a boy's entire right arm.

He is crew-cut Army, sits in the attached row across from me,
feet up on a digicam rucksack. It's probably Bible, that tattoo,

John or Luke, maybe Timothy, and the boy is beautiful, the boy
is totally unmarred but for his tattoo. When he flips his cell phone

open & shut, open & shut, I want to reach out to stroke his
wheat-colored stubble, ask him what his black ink means.

Portare, to bear. *I still have many things to say to you,*
but you cannot bear them now. Portare bellum: to carry the war.

Before Thanksgiving, we will pull in to the Sunoco off I-78 in Jersey,
where one veteran in hunting camo carries another like a bride

over a threshold. They will be laughing when they chime
through the door of the Quik-Mart. Every footstep and palm-press.

Every machine propelling us forward. Wrecked amen of beverage cases,
clicking gas pumps. Selah hallelujah. *And I will carry you away*

beyond Babylon, a passage, portare, to bear from one place to another,
on one's arms, head, or back. Our bodies bear witness (to the light

to the darkness), bear fruit (lucky lucky), bear the sins of many,
bear whatever it is into the distance. When our neighbor dies—

the pastor's wife—he calls over, asks me to go through her clothes,
take them home. She would want you to have them, he says.

*For we brought nothing into this world, and it is certain we can carry
nothing out* (except our stories). In this story, the door jingles hello.

The man being carried turns his head toward me,
over the shoulder of the man carrying him, and he is laughing.

The word I thought of was mirth: *and Sarah laughed
to herself, and God asked Abraham, Why did Sarah laugh?*

Porto. I bring my son inside by the hand, after them.
He has to pee. The bathroom is outside. There is no key,

says the cashier, and I see the laughing man balanced on a stool
at the counter, which is when I notice that he has no legs.

His buddy peruses the beef jerky aisle, and when he turns,
one side of his face is scarred and pitted. The bathroom

is fetid. My small son touches the graffitied tiles,
the toilet seat, asks about the condom machine

bolted to the wall, and I stumble through some answer
about adult things, about protection. He does not ask

about the soldier with no legs. Portant. They carry.
Outside, their pickup is filled with hunting gear,

camo tarps, a wheelchair, a USMC sticker. Portavi.
I have carried my son and I will not bear another one.

My neighbor's name was Ruth, and before she died I was often
tempted to ask her to pray for me, as if Jesus could cure

our secondary infertility. That story of him touching the bier.
Then the bearers stood still. And he said, "Young man, get up."

And he told the mother not to weep, and her only son sat up,
began to speak. Portamus. You & I, we carry the burden together

of the not-exactly-barren. We were fruitful and now un-,
and some days we are so old that the gray in your hair

gleams like treasure, and others we are so young I get carded
for beer at the Food Lion. In this story, I put off visiting

the neighbor's to go through Ruth's clothes, and instead
get her back issues of *Good Housekeeping* from her husband.

In my story, your face is turned toward me, and we are laughing
at the ancient recipes, and in my story everyone is marked

and we all carry, have been carried, bear up under the weight
of our dead and our living and our injured and injured and injured.

Daily, we bear the weight of more weight forward;
portare is hardly ever said of a light load.

NOTES

The title *Copia* was taken from photographer Brian Ulrich's photography project of the same name (notifbutwhen.com).

"Retail Space Available" and "Ghostbox" were based on interviews with photographer Brian Ulrich, about his experiences photographing sites for his project *Dark Stores, Ghost Boxes, and Dead Malls.*

"with/out" is after Janice N. Harrington's poem "Heat," from her book *Even the Hollow My Body Made Is Gone* (BOA Editions, 2007).

Both "Niagara" poems are based on images from the photo series of the same name, by Alec Soth (alecsoth.com/photography/projects/niagra/), as well as interviews with the photographer about his experiences on the project.

Some of the phrases in "Let the future begin this way:" were taken from photographer Danny Lyon's book *Pictures from the New World* (Aperture, 1988) and *The New American Ghetto* by photographer Camilo José Vergara (Rutgers University Press, 1997). The last four lines are from Romans 10:15.

The Yiddish lines in "Yiddishland" come from *Di folks-shprakh*, by Y. Klepfish (Warsaw: Farlag "Progress," 1909–1910) as cited in *Adventures in Yiddishland* by Jeffrey Shandler (University of California Press, 2006).

"To Whom It May Concern:" contains language from an NPR story by Daniel Zwerdling, called "A Bright Spot of Life on the Icy Continent" (March 15, 2008).

"The Book of Dissolution" was inspired by James Griffioen's photographs and account of his explorations of the former Detroit Public Schools Book Depository/Roosevelt Warehouse, as recounted on his blog (www.sweet-juniper.com).

"Post-Industrialization," "All That Blue Fire," "Outside the Abandoned Packard Plant," "And After the Ark," "Inside the Frame," "Outside the Frame," and "Borderama" were commissioned by *Virginia Quarterly Review* for the Spring 2011 issue, entitled *Ruin & Rebirth*. These documentary poems resulted from a reporting trip to Detroit with Jesse

Dukes and Kate Ringo in August 2010, and would not exist had it not been for their hard work on the project, and the support of Ted Genoways. There are many other Detroit residents who gave us their time, stories, and expertise, for which I'm grateful: Dan Austin, Terry Blackhawk, Alvin Brewer, Delores Casey, Arnold Collens, Sean Doerr, Wendy Ford, Oren Goldenberg, Vicki Hooks Green, Lolita Hernandez, Jerry Herron, Greg Lenhoff, Andy Linn, Emily Linn, Peter Markus, Joan Nash, Suzanne Scarfone, Nick Tobier, Stuart Trager, and Shar Willis.

"Porto, Portare, Portavi, Portatus" contains lines from John 16:12, Acts 7:43, 1 Timothy 6:7, Genesis 18:12, and Luke 7:14.

Acknowledgments

I am grateful to all the editors of the following journals and anthologies where these poems, sometimes in different form, first appeared:

AGNI: "The Book of Dissolution," "Niagara";
Anti-: "with/out";
Cave Wall: "Ars Poetica with Radio Apparatus, Toddler, & Ducks";
Cellpoems: "And the moon";
Crab Orchard Review: "Maple Ridge";
Gulf Coast: "Staking a Claim";
Handsome: "Interrobang," "Retail Space Available";
The Ilanot Review: "You return the Torah to the ark," "By Other Means";
Indiana Review: "Niagara," "Yiddishland";
jubilat: "Let the future begin this way:";
Ninth Letter: "Terra Nullius";
Painted Bride Quarterly: "Inconsequential Alchemy";
Ploughshares: "Porto, Portare, Portavi, Portatus";
Plume: "And After the Ark," "Apologetics";
River Styx: "Snowpocalypse";
The Rumpus: "Walmart Supercenter";
Salt Hill: "Ghostbox";
Slate.com: "Big Box Encounter";
The Southern Review: "The Language of Happiness," "Correspondence," "In/exhaustible";
Sou'wester: "Maple Ridge";
Subtropics: "To Whom It May Concern";
Tin House: "Terra Nullius";
Virginia Quarterly Review: "Post-Industrialization," "All That Blue Fire," "Borderama," "Outside the Abandoned Packard Plant," "Inside the Frame," "Outside the Frame";
Waccamaw: "The Architecture of Memory";
Whiskey Island: "One Version of December."

"Litany of our Radical Engagement with the Material World" was first published in *Alhambra Poetry Calendar 2011*.

"Untitled [and the moon]" was first published on the Academy of American Poets website.

"Yizker Bukh" was first published on *The Chronicle of Higher Education* "Arts & Academe" blog, and reprinted in *The Hide-and-Seek Muse: Annotations of Contemporary Poetry*, Ed. Lisa Russ Spaar (Drunken Boat Media, 2013).

"Yiddishland" was reprinted in *The Bloomsbury Anthology of Contemporary Jewish American Poetry*, Eds. Matthew Silverman and Deborah Ager (Bloomsbury Academic, 2013).

Many thanks to Virginia Tech (in particular, the Department of English, and the College of Liberal Arts and Human Sciences) and the Virginia Center for the Creative Arts, for time and space and support. I'm grateful to the Child Development Center for Learning and Research (CDCLR) at Virginia Tech, and Rainbow Riders Childcare Center, for joyfully teaching and tending to my children, which allowed me to write this book. I am also indebted to agent extraordinaire Nat Jacks at Inkwell Management, and the poets who helped me with this manuscript in its various stages: Sandra Beasley, Mary Biddinger, Jehanne Dubrow, Tom Gardner, Joy Katz, David Stack, Susan Somers-Willett, and Rachel Zucker—their big hearts and eagle eyes. Peter Conners and the fine folks at BOA Editions, Ltd. are the tops.

And always, Steve Trost—love, lynchpin, lyre, lookout.

About the Author

Erika Meitner's first collection of poems, *Inventory at the All-Night Drugstore*, won the 2002 Anhinga-Robert Dana Prize for Poetry from Anhinga Press. Her second collection, *Ideal Cities*, was a winner of the 2009 National Poetry Series Award and was published by HarperCollins in 2010. Her next book, *Makeshift Instructions for Vigilant Girls*, was published by Anhinga Press in 2011. She is a graduate of Dartmouth College and the MFA program at the University of Virginia, where she was a Henry Hoyns Fellow, and also earned an M.A. in Religion as a Morgenstern Fellow in Jewish Studies. Her work has appeared in *American Poetry Review*, *The Best American Poetry 2011*, *Gulf Coast*, *Ploughshares*, *Best African American Essays 2010*, *Tin House*, and *Prairie Schooner*, among other journals and anthologies. She is currently an associate professor of English at Virginia Tech, where she teaches in the MFA program.

BOA Editions, Ltd. American Poets Continuum Series

Colophon

BOA Editions, Ltd., a not-for-profit publisher of poetry and other literary works, fosters readership and appreciation of contemporary literature. By identifying, cultivating, and publishing both new and established poets and selecting authors of unique literary talent, BOA brings high-quality literature to the public. Support for this effort comes from the sale of its publications, grant funding, and private donations.

The publication of this book is made possible, in part,
by the special support of the following individuals:

Anonymous x 4
Armbruster Family Foundation
Jeanne Marie Beaumont
Bernadette Catalana, *in memory of Irving Pheterson*
Anne Germanacos
Carla Giambrone, Giampro Corporation
Suzanne Gouvernet
Melissa Hall & Joe Torre
Michael Hall
X. J. & Dorothy M. Kennedy
Jack & Gail Langerak
Barbara & John Lovenheim
Edith Matthai, *in memory of Peter Hursh*
Boo Poulin
Cindy Winetroub Rogers
Deborah Ronnen & Sherman Levey
Steven O. Russell & Phyllis Rifkin-Russell
Michael Waters & Mihaela Moscaliuc